THIS BOOK BELONGS TO

....

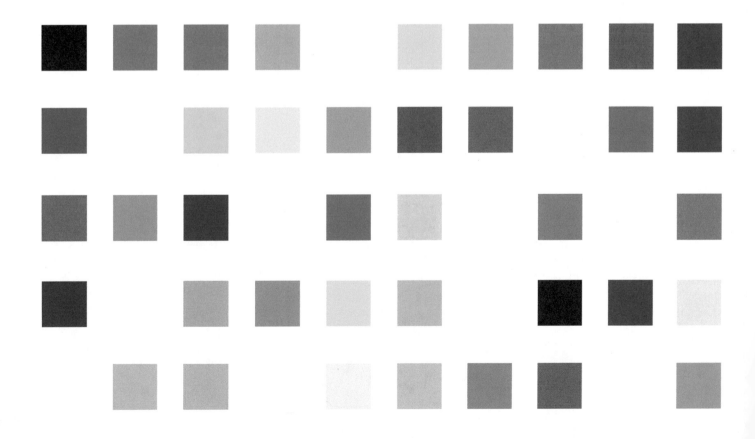

THREE SPARROWS

MAKE YOUR OWN MULTIPLICATION AND DIVISION GALLERY!

CONTENTS:

MULTIPLICATION CHART 1-100

x	1	2	3	4	5	6	7	8	9	10
1	1	2	3	4	5	6	7	8	9	10
2	2	4	6	8	10	12	14	16	18	20
3	3	6	9	12	15	18	21	24	27	30
4	4	8	12	16	20	24	28	32	36	40
5	5	10	15	20	25	30	35	40	45	50
6	6	12	18	24	30	36	42	48	54	60
7	7	14	21	28	35	42	49	56	63	70
8	8	16	24	32	40	48	56	64	72	80
9	9	18	27	36	45	54	63	72	81	90
10	10	20	30	40	50	60	70	80	90	100

Color by number: multiplication by 2

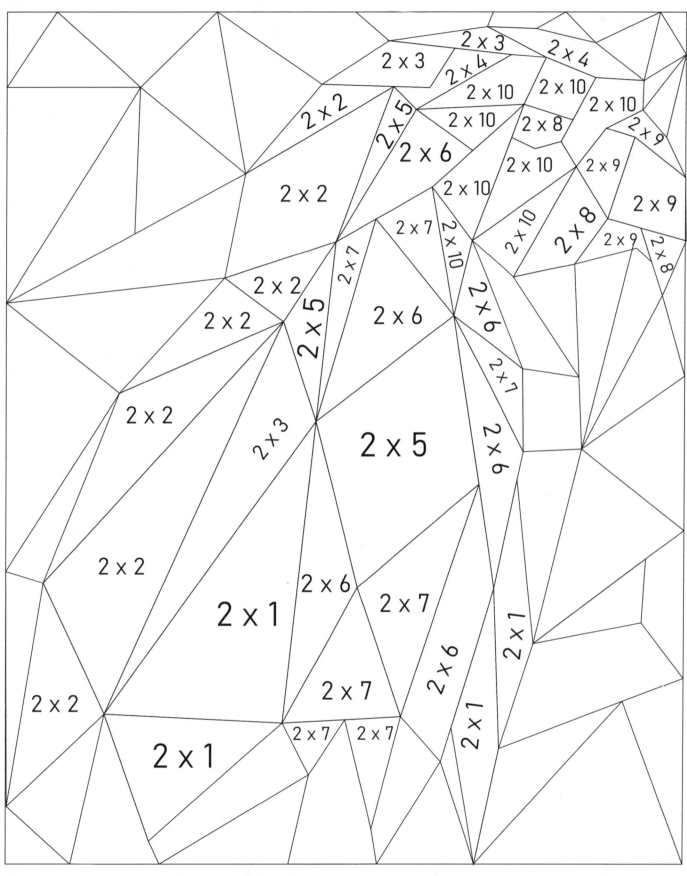

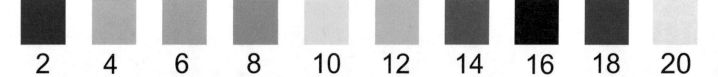

| 2 | 4 | 6 | 8 | 10 | 12 | 14 | 16 | 18 | 20 |

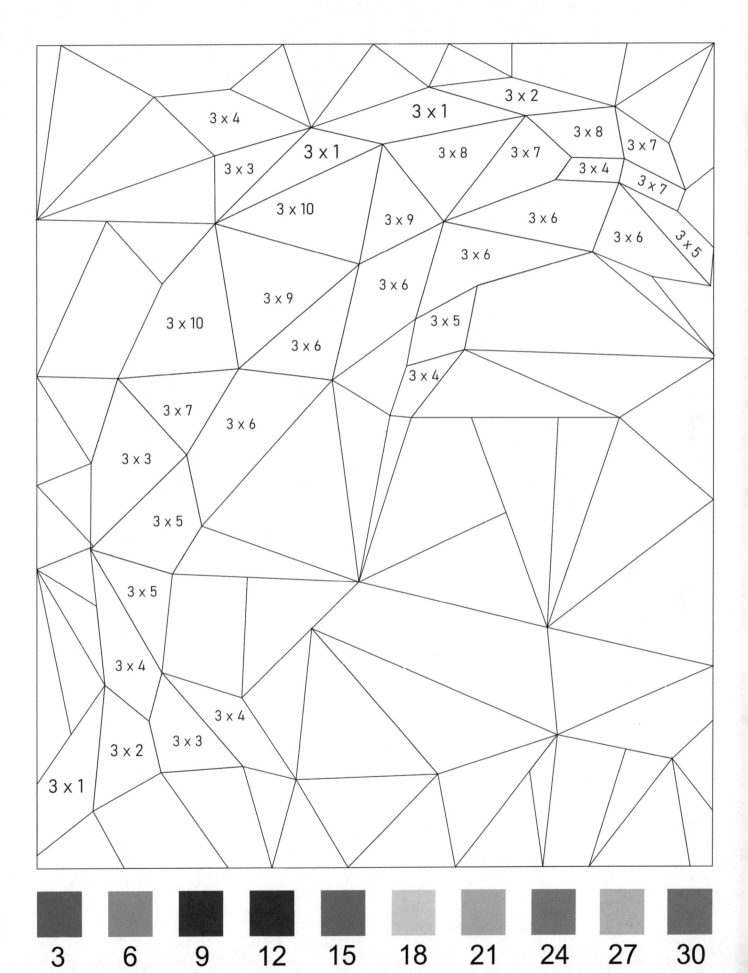

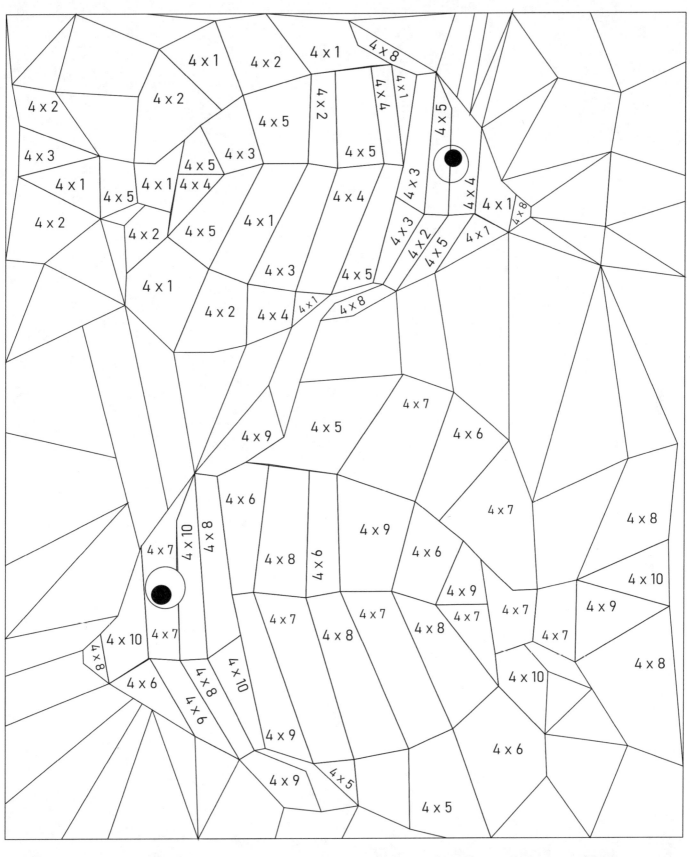

| 4 | 8 | 12 | 16 | 20 | 24 | 28 | 32 | 36 | 40 |

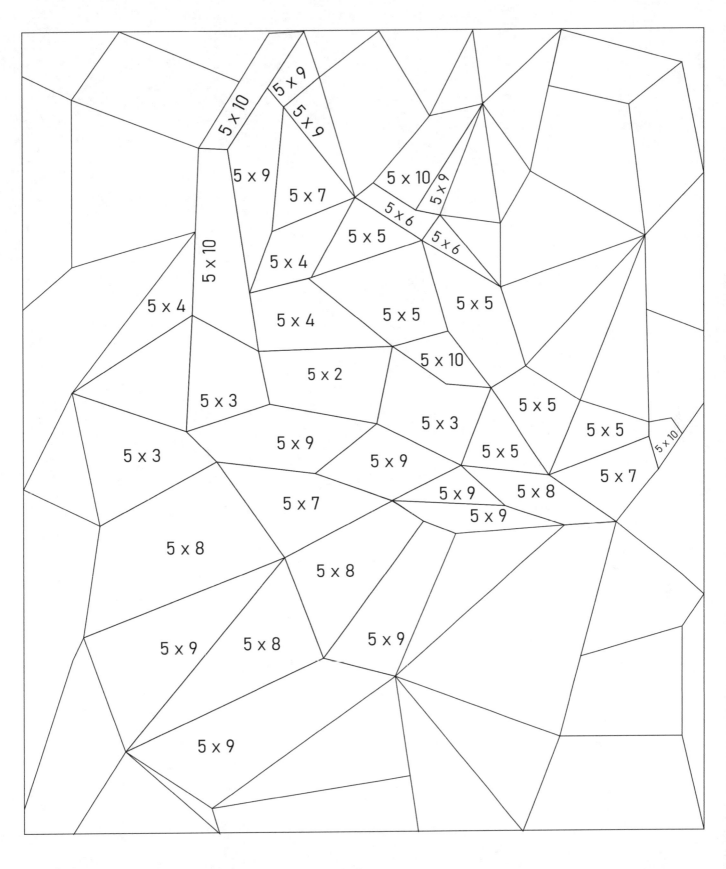

5 x 10
5 x 9
5 x 9
5 x 9
5 x 7
5 x 10
5 x 9
5 x 6
5 x 5
5 x 6
5 x 10
5 x 4
5 x 4
5 x 5
5 x 5
5 x 4
5 x 4
5 x 5
5 x 2
5 x 10
5 x 3
5 x 3
5 x 5
5 x 9
5 x 5
5 x 5
5 x 3
5 x 9
5 x 5
5 x 10
5 x 8
5 x 7
5 x 9
5 x 7
5 x 9
5 x 8
5 x 5
5 x 8
5 x 8
5 x 9
5 x 8
5 x 9
5 x 9

 10 **15** **20** **25** **30** **35** **40** **45** **50**

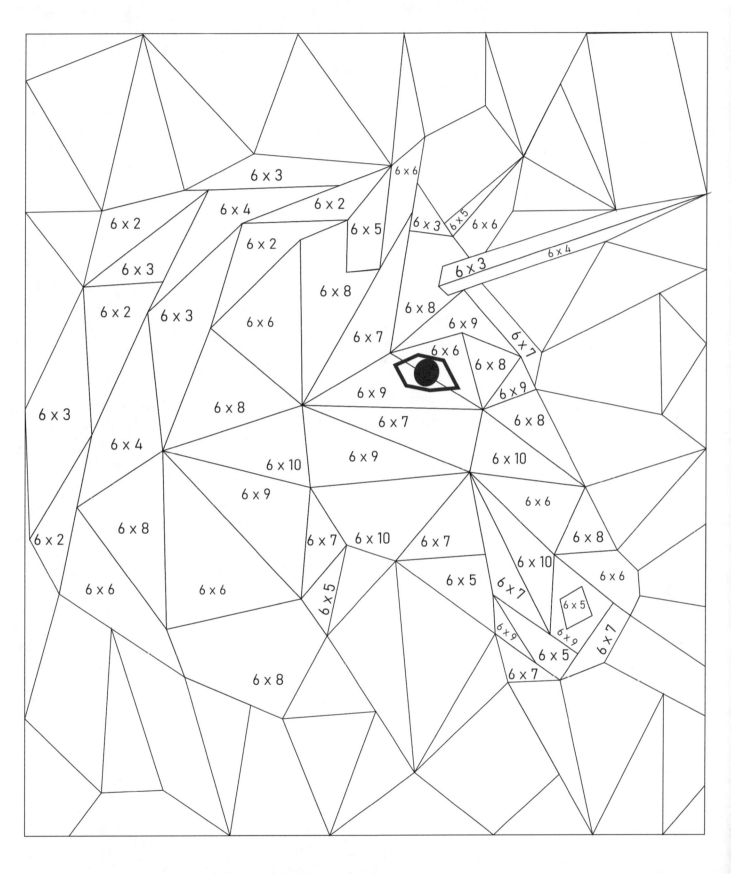

 12
 18
 24
 30
 36
 42
 48
 54
 60

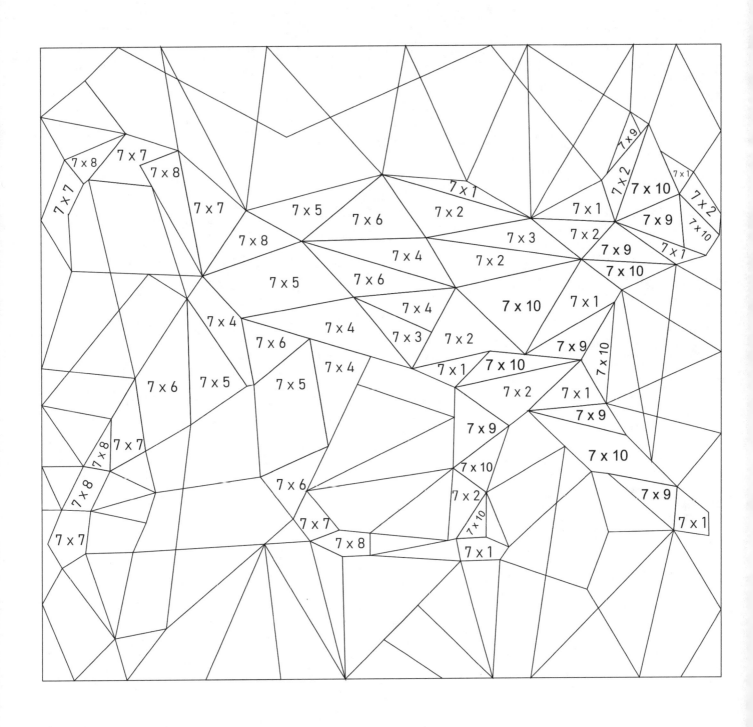

| 7 | 14 | 21 | 28 | 35 | 42 | 49 | 56 | 63 | 70 |

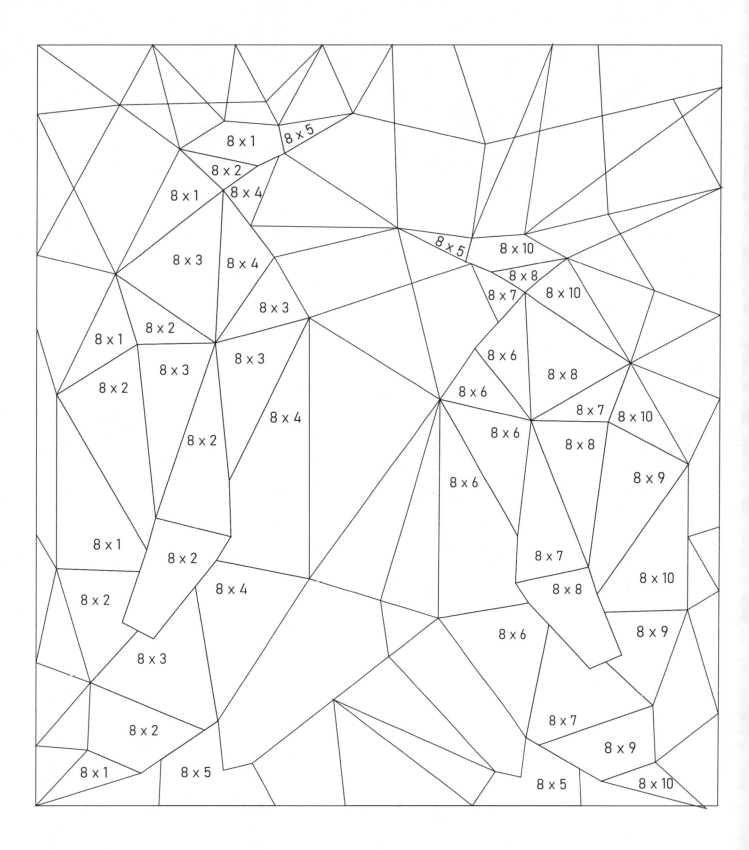

 8
 16
 24
 32
 40
 48
 56
 64
 72
 80

 9
 18
 27
 36
 45
 54
 63
 72
 81
90

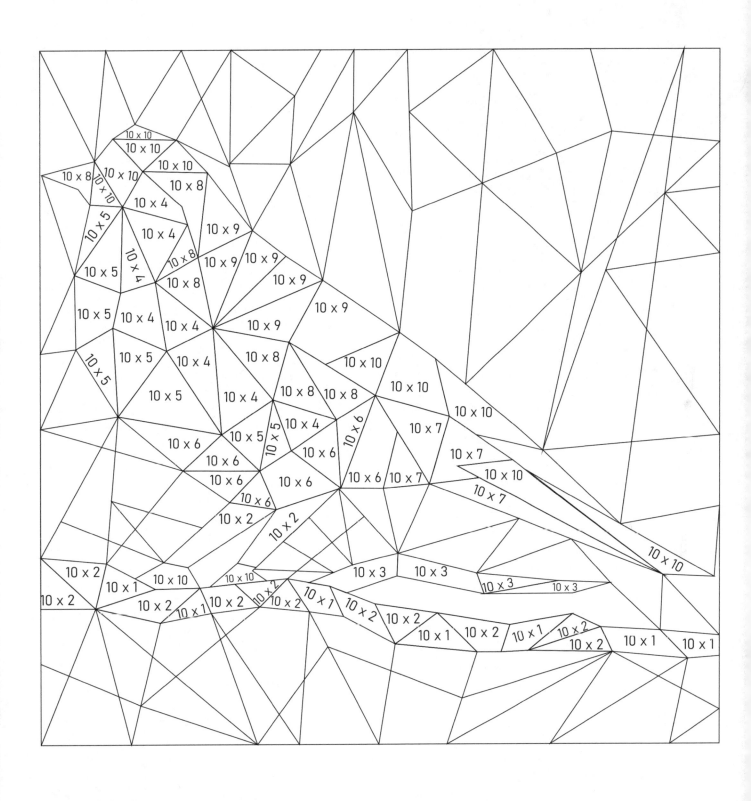

| 10 | 20 | 30 | 40 | 50 | 60 | 70 | 80 | 90 | 100 |

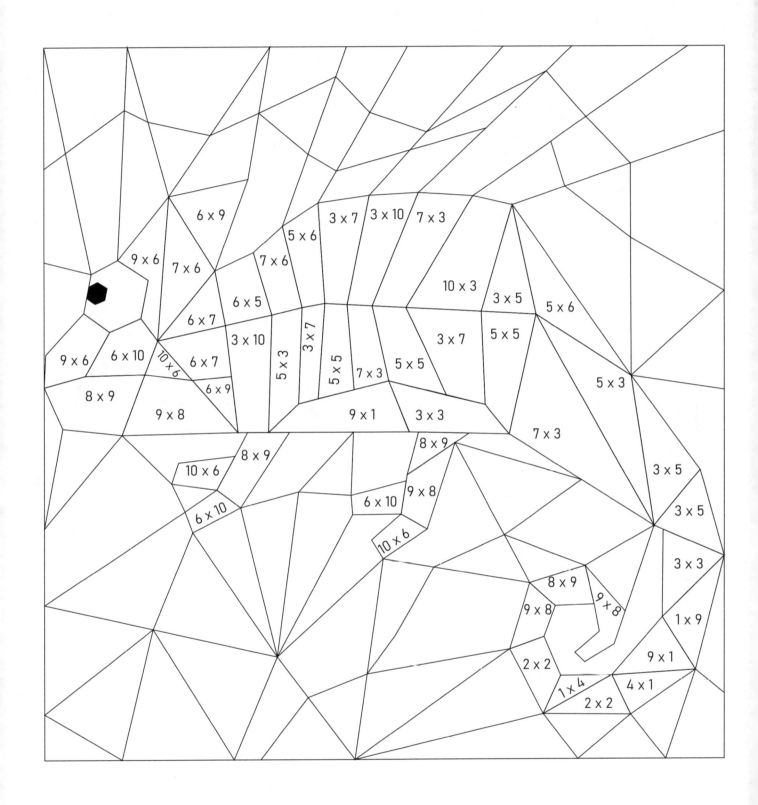

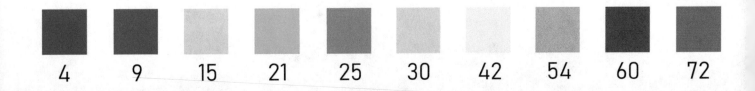

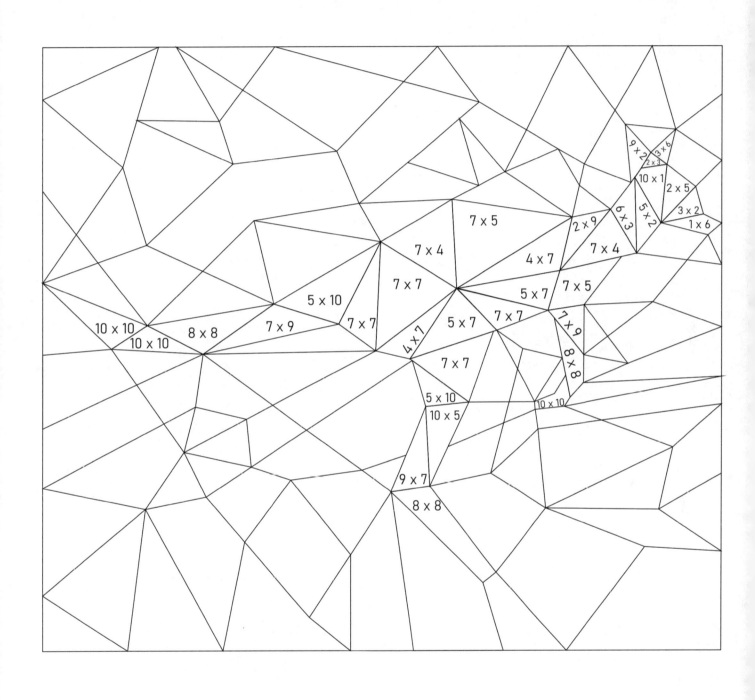

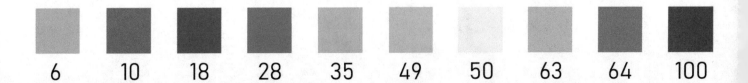

| 6 | 10 | 18 | 28 | 35 | 49 | 50 | 63 | 64 | 100 |

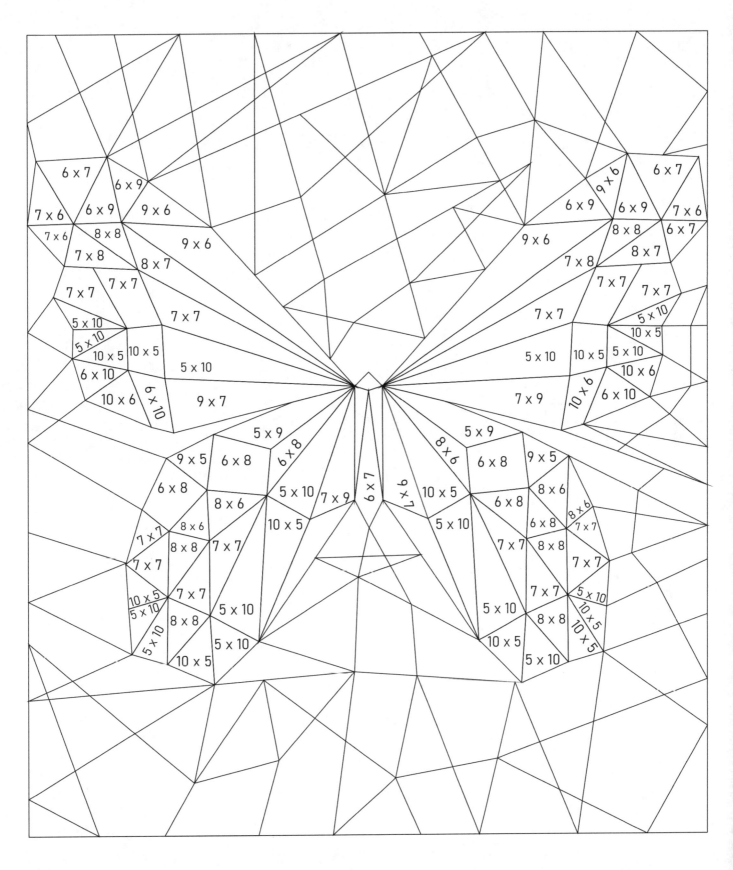

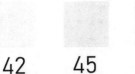 42   45   48   49   50   54   56   60   63   64

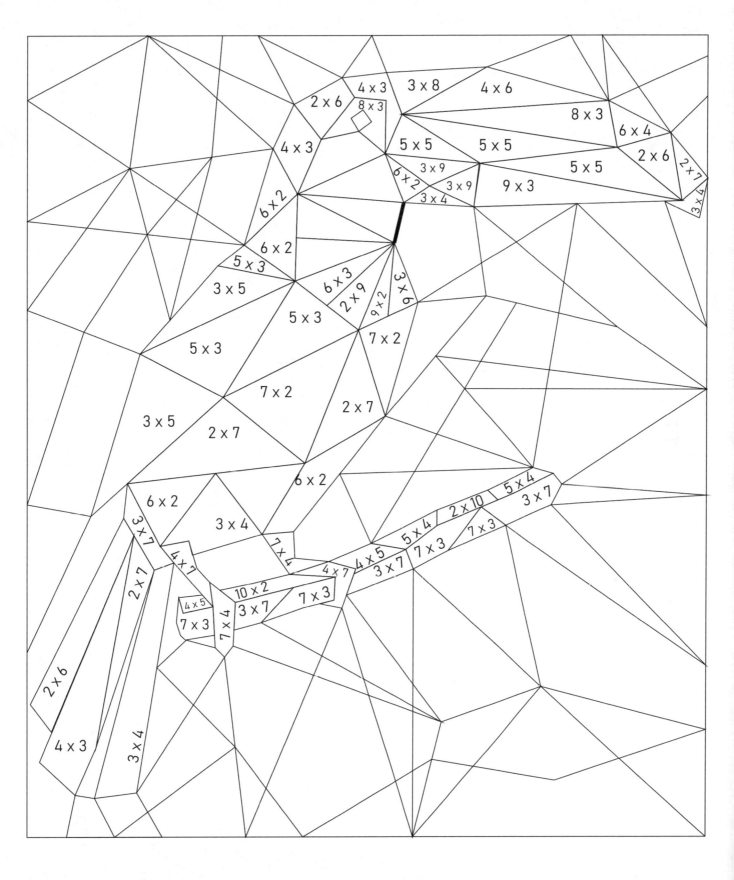

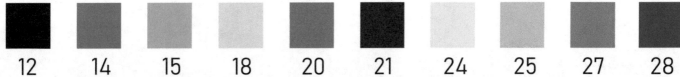

12	14	15	18	20	21	24	25	27	28

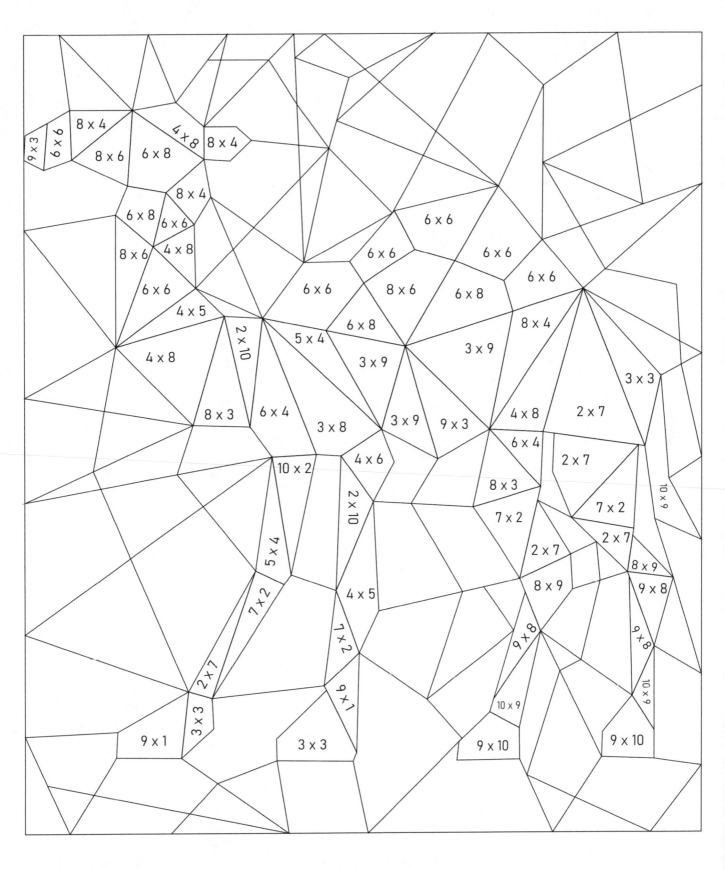

      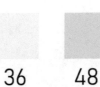

| 9 | 14 | 20 | 24 | 27 | 32 | 36 | 48 | 72 | 90 |

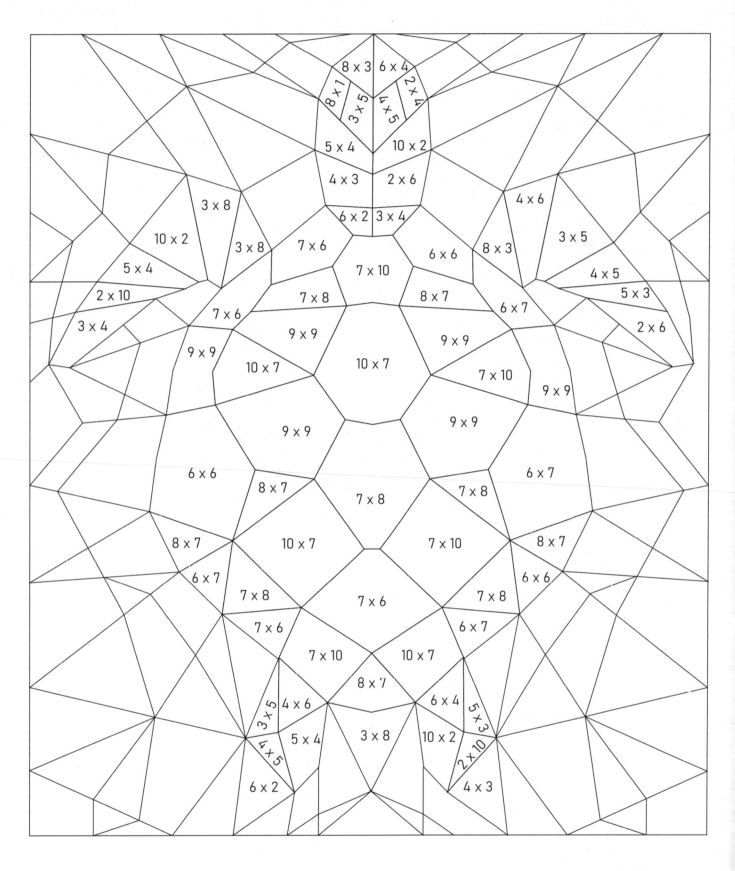

 8
 12
 15
 20
 24
 36
 42
 56
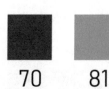 70 81

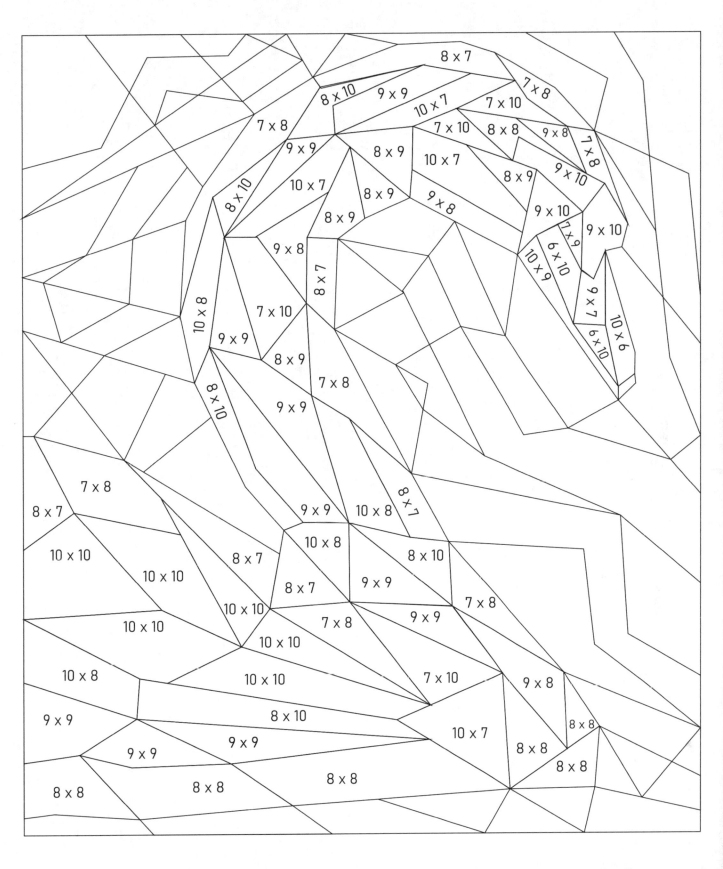

| 56 | 60 | 63 | 64 | 70 | 72 | 80 | 81 | 90 | 100 |

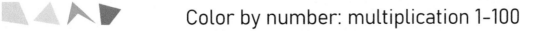

| 30 | 32 | 35 | 36 | 40 | 42 | 45 | 48 | 50 | 54 |

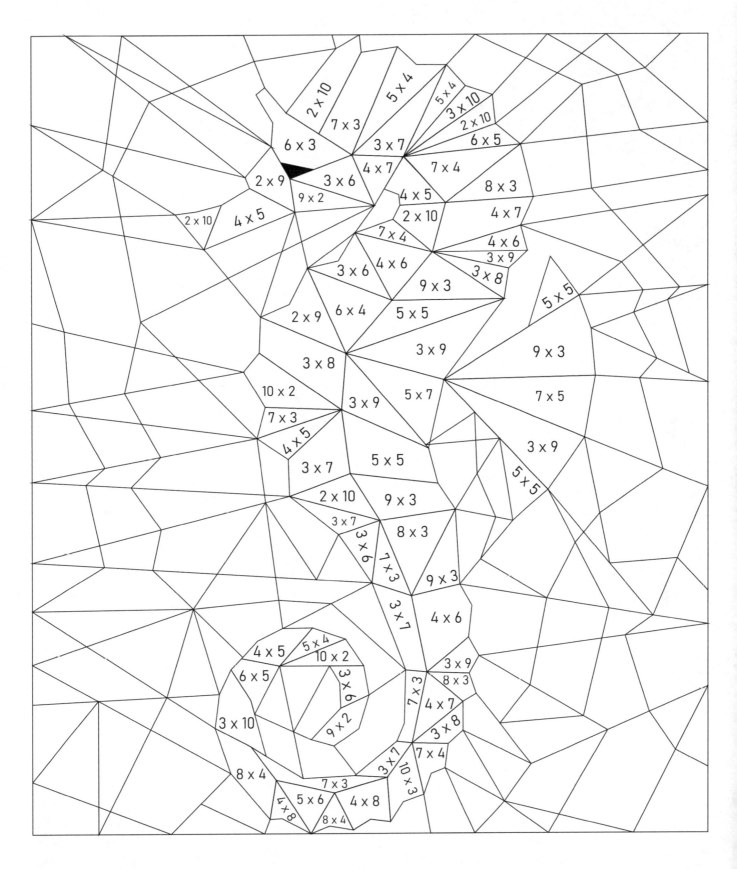

 18
 20
 21
 24
25
27
 28
 30
 32
 35

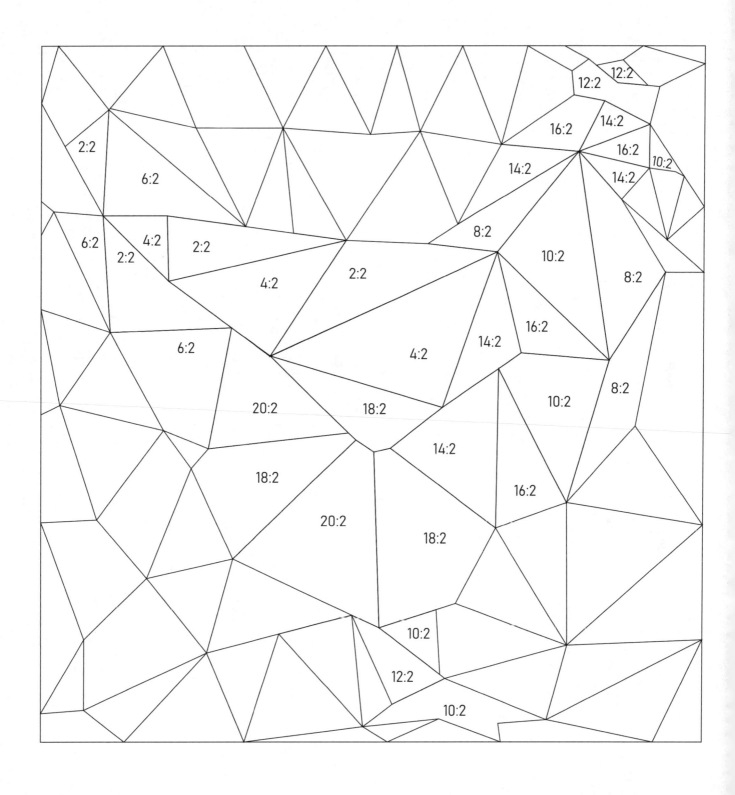

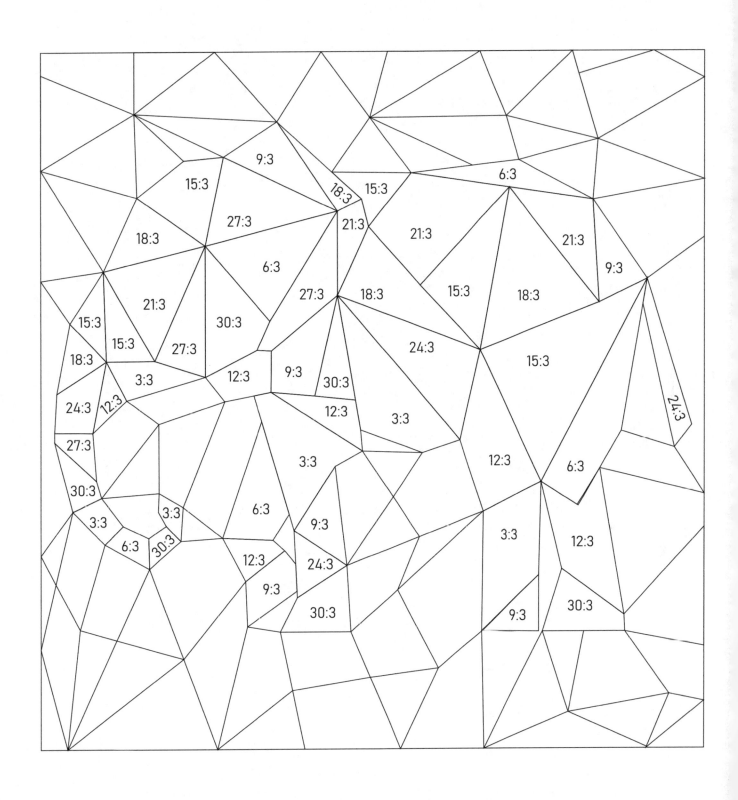

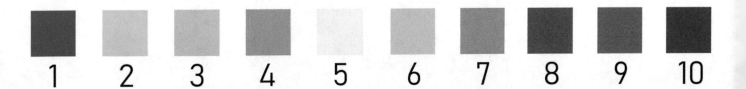

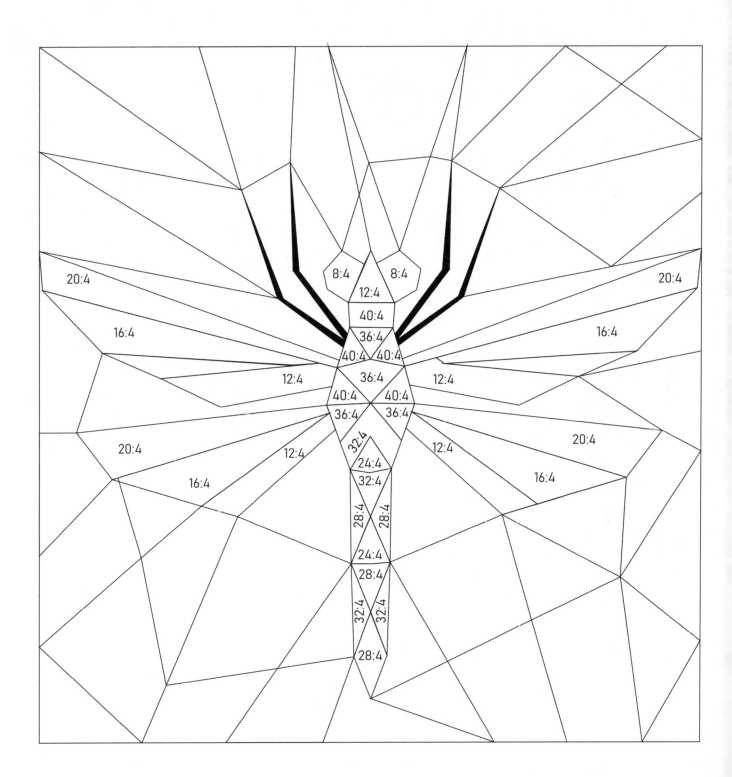

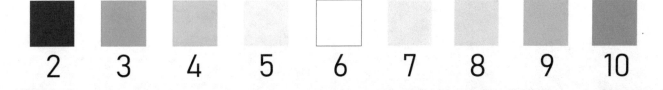

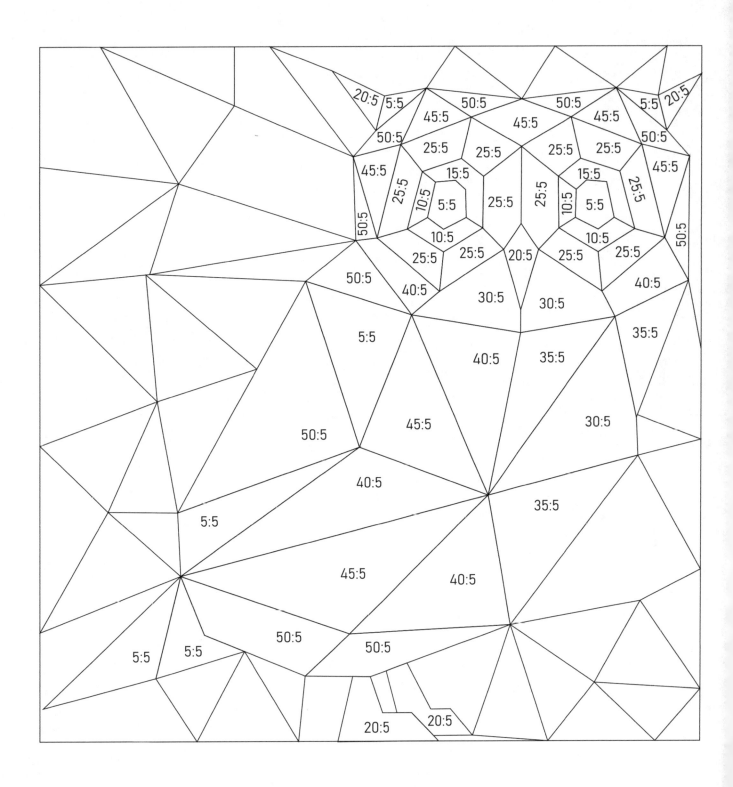

Color by number: division by 6

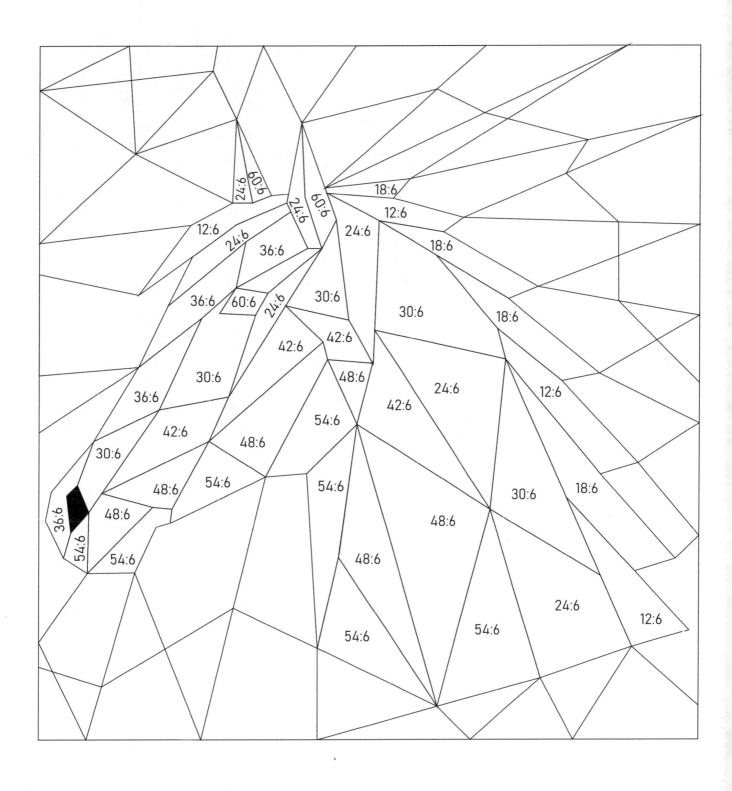

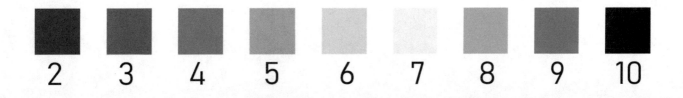

| 2 | 3 | 4 | 5 | 6 | 7 | 8 | 9 | 10 |

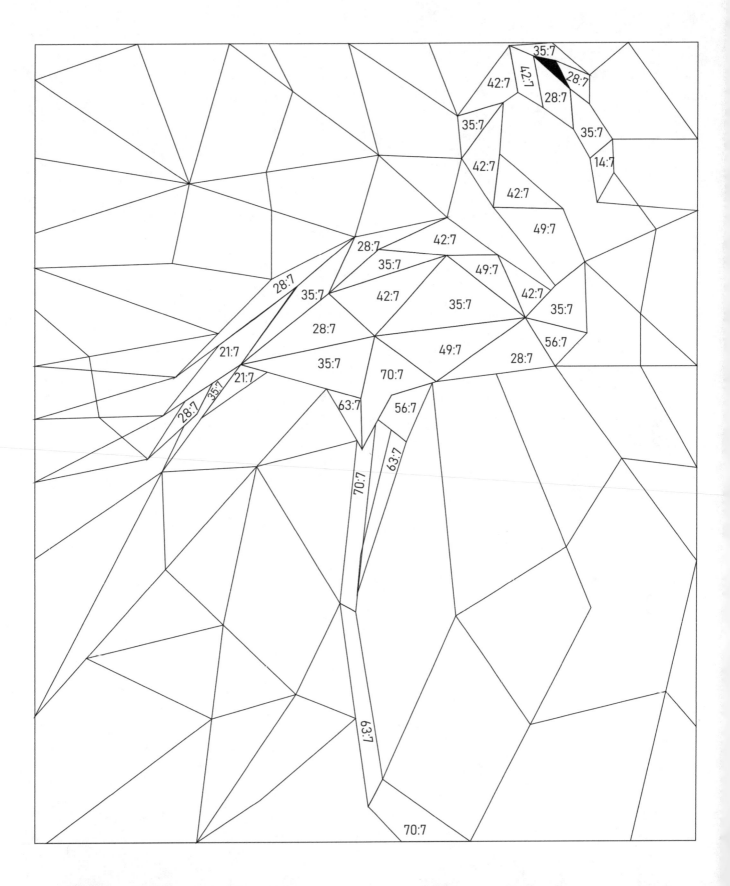

Color by number: division by 8

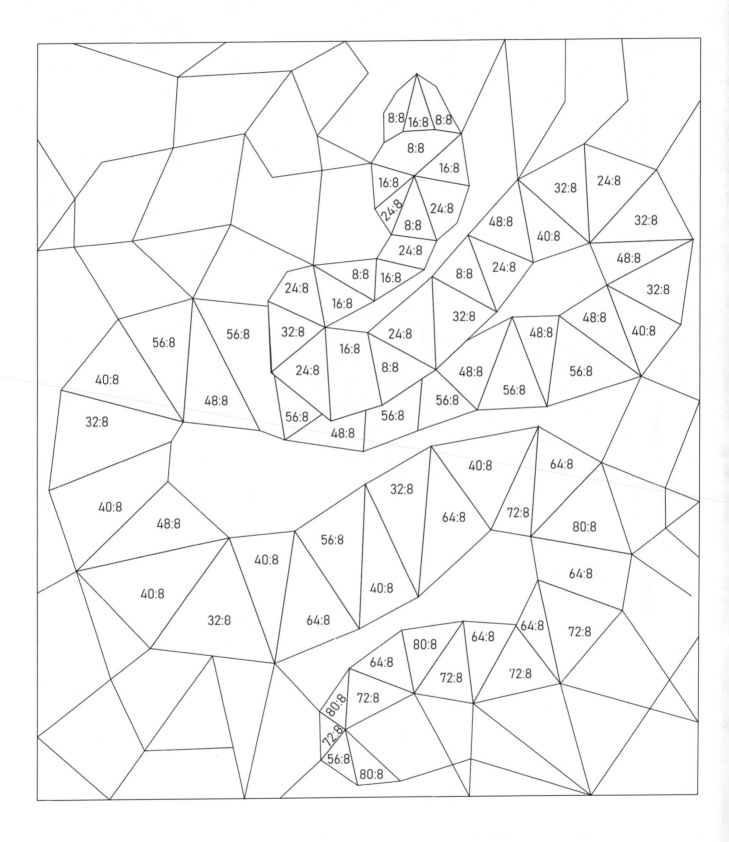

8:8 16:8 8:8
8:8
16:8
16:8
24:8 24:8
8:8
24:8
24:8 8:8 16:8
16:8
32:8 24:8
24:8 16:8
56:8 56:8
32:8
40:8 48:8
32:8
56:8
48:8
56:8 48:8
32:8 24:8
8:8
32:8
48:8
24:8
40:8
48:8
32:8
48:8
40:8
48:8
56:8
48:8 56:8
56:8
56:8 48:8
40:8 64:8
32:8
40:8
48:8
32:8
64:8
72:8
80:8
64:8
56:8
40:8
40:8
40:8
32:8
64:8
40:8
64:8
64:8 64:8
80:8 72:8
64:8
72:8 72:8
80:8
72:8
72:8
80:8
72:8
56:8
80:8

 1
2 3
 4 5
 6 7
 8 9 10

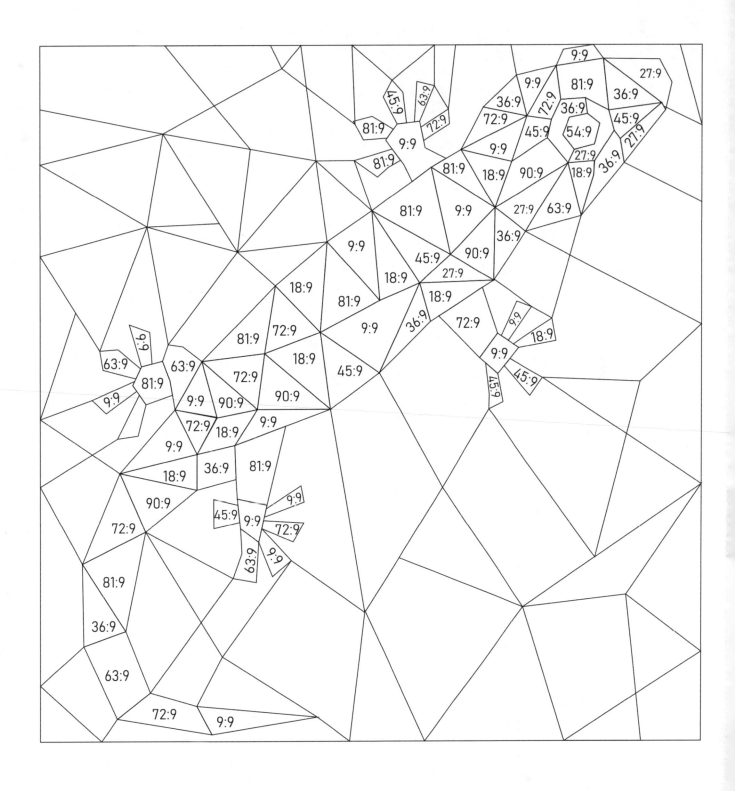

1 2 3 4 5 6 7 8 9 10

Color by number: division by 10

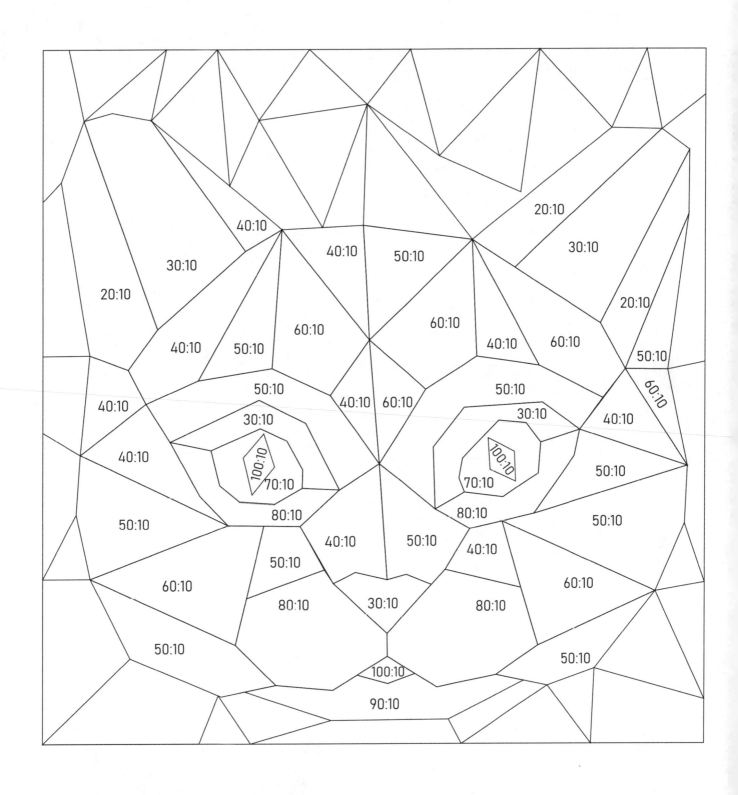

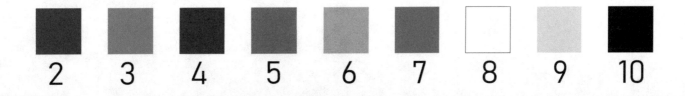

SOLUTIONS: MULTIPLICATION LEVEL 1

Color by number: multiplication by 2

| 2 | 4 | 6 | 8 | 10 | 12 | 14 | 16 | 18 | 20 |

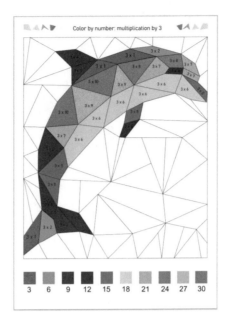

Color by number: multiplication by 3

| 3 | 6 | 9 | 12 | 15 | 18 | 21 | 24 | 27 | 30 |

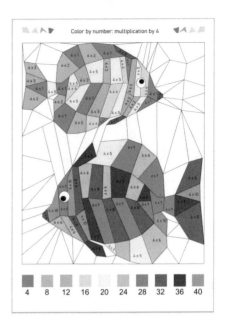

Color by number: multiplication by 4

| 4 | 8 | 12 | 16 | 20 | 24 | 28 | 32 | 36 | 40 |

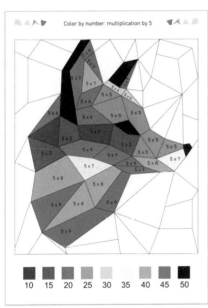

Color by number: multiplication by 5

| 10 | 15 | 20 | 25 | 30 | 35 | 40 | 45 | 50 |

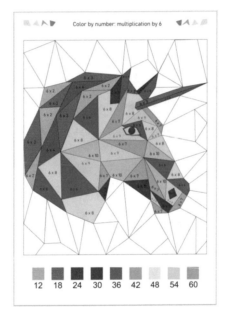

Color by number: multiplication by 6

| 12 | 18 | 24 | 30 | 36 | 42 | 48 | 54 | 60 |

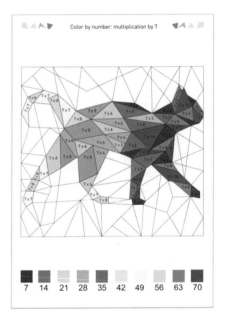

Color by number: multiplication by 7

| 7 | 14 | 21 | 28 | 35 | 42 | 49 | 56 | 63 | 70 |

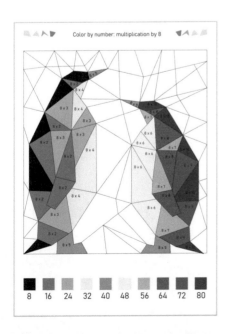

Color by number: multiplication by 8

| 8 | 16 | 24 | 32 | 40 | 48 | 56 | 64 | 72 | 80 |

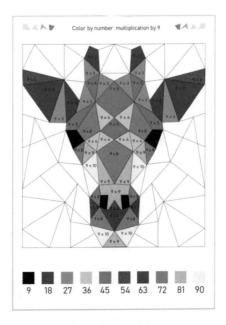

Color by number: multiplication by 9

| 9 | 18 | 27 | 36 | 45 | 54 | 63 | 72 | 81 | 90 |

Color by number: multiplication by 10

| 10 | 20 | 30 | 40 | 50 | 60 | 70 | 80 | 90 | 100 |

SOLUTIONS: MULTIPLICATION LEVEL 2

| 4 | 9 | 15 | 21 | 25 | 30 | 42 | 54 | 60 | 72 |

| 6 | 10 | 18 | 28 | 35 | 49 | 50 | 63 | 64 | 100 |

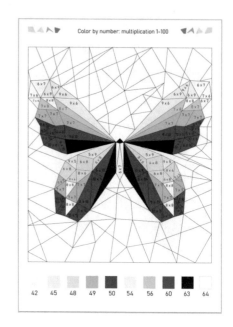

| 42 | 45 | 48 | 49 | 50 | 54 | 56 | 60 | 63 | 64 |

| 12 | 14 | 15 | 18 | 20 | 21 | 24 | 25 | 27 | 28 |

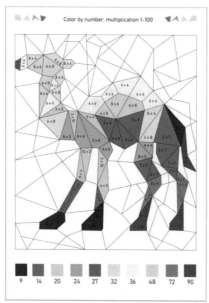

| 9 | 14 | 20 | 24 | 27 | 32 | 36 | 48 | 72 | 90 |

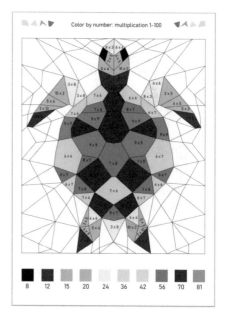

| 8 | 12 | 15 | 20 | 24 | 36 | 42 | 56 | 70 | 81 |

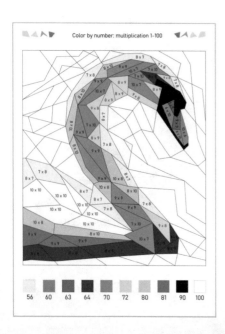

| 56 | 60 | 63 | 64 | 70 | 72 | 80 | 81 | 90 | 100 |

| 30 | 32 | 35 | 36 | 40 | 42 | 45 | 48 | 50 | 54 |

| 18 | 20 | 21 | 24 | 25 | 27 | 28 | 30 | 32 | 35 |

SOLUTIONS: DIVISION

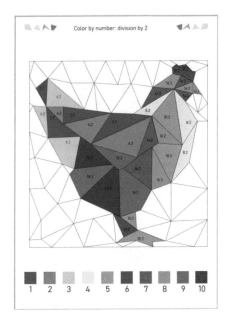

Color by number: division by 2

1 2 3 4 5 6 7 8 9 10

Color by number: division by 3

1 2 3 4 5 6 7 8 9 10

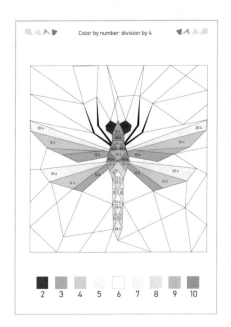

Color by number: division by 4

2 3 4 5 6 7 8 9 10

Color by number: division by 5

1 2 3 4 5 6 7 8 9 10

Color by number: division by 6

2 3 4 5 6 7 8 9 10

Color by number: division by 7

2 3 4 5 6 7 8 9 10

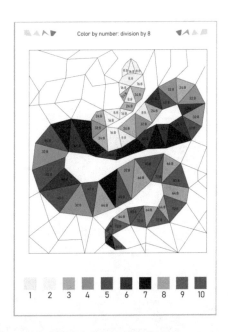

Color by number: division by 8

1 2 3 4 5 6 7 8 9 10

Color by number: division by 9

1 2 3 4 5 6 7 8 9 10

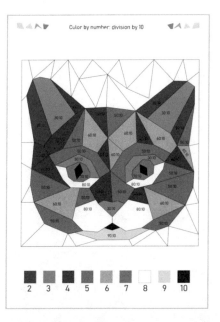

Color by number: division by 10

2 3 4 5 6 7 8 9 10

Color by multiplication as in the example

1 x 3

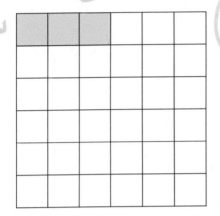

1 x 3 = 3

4 x 3

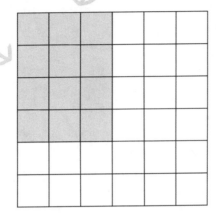

4 x 3 = 12

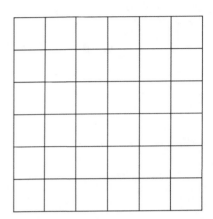

2 x 5 = ...

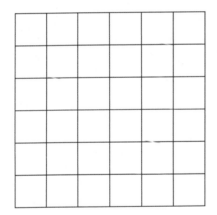

4 x 5 = ...

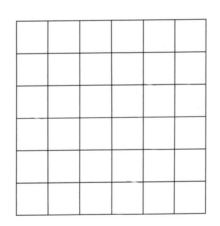

2 x 6 = ...

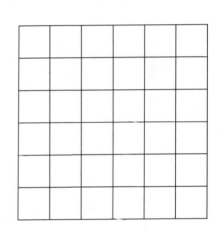

5 x 5 = ...

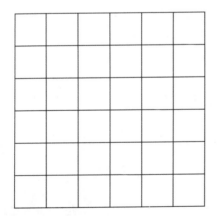

3 x 6 = ...

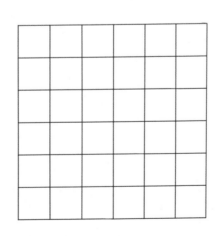

6 x 5 = ...

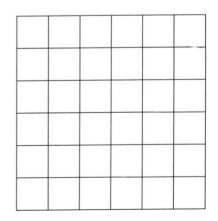

3 x 2 = ...

Math crossword puzzle

Fill in the blanks of each crossword puzzle
to make the multiplication equations true.

			x		=	72		
x		x						x
2	x		=	4		5		2
=		=		x		x		=
10		16		3	x	6	=	
				=		=		
	x	2	=					

	x	2	=	
x		x		
4	x	7	=	
=		=		
24				

30:5	14:7	40:4	28:7
24:2	40:8	42:6	15:5
81:9	8:8	33:3	40:5

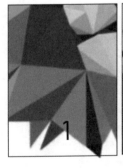

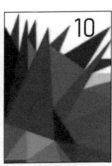

Math crossword puzzle

Fill in the blanks of each crossword puzzle
to make the division equations true.

Top-left grid

40	÷		=	4
÷				÷
	÷		=	2
=				=
5		÷		=	6

Top-right grid

	÷	4	=	9
÷				÷
	÷	2	=	
=				=
				3

Lower grid

÷			
4	÷	2	=	
=			
	÷	1	=	

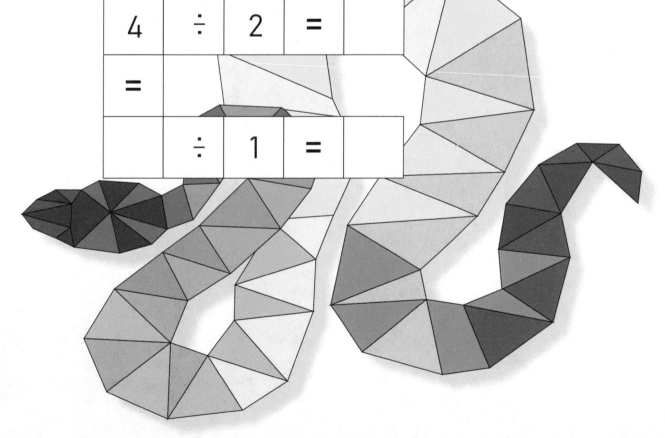

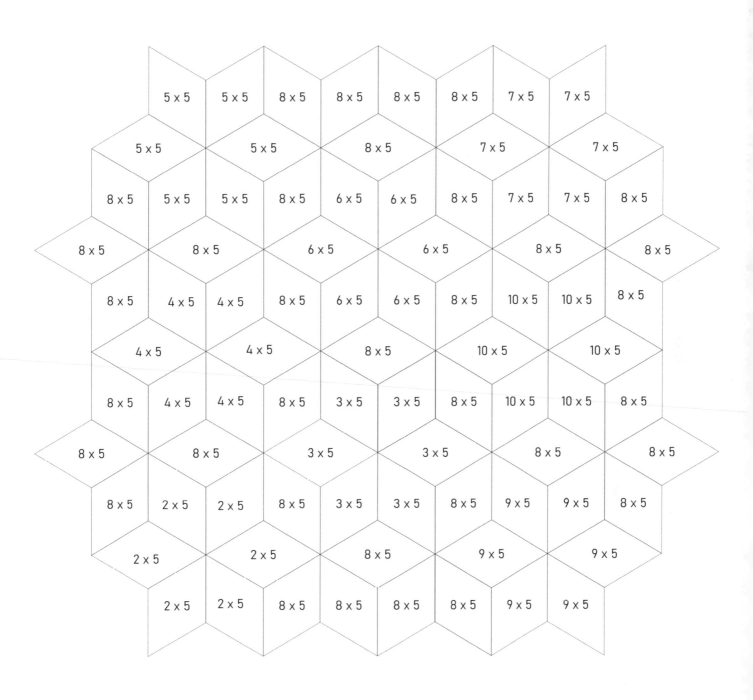

| 10 | 15 | 20 | 25 | 30 | 35 | 40 | 45 | 50 |

Thank you for purchasing our book „Color by Math: Multiplication and Division for kids ages 8-12". We hope your child had a great time solving problems, coloring, and discovering the fascinating world of multiplication. Your support is a huge motivation for us to create even more educational materials to help children develop their skills.

If you were satisfied with our book, we encourage you to leave a review on Amazon so that other parents can learn about our product. Your opinion is invaluable to us.

If you have any questions, comments, or suggestions, please don't hesitate to contact us at the email address: threesparrows@gmail.com . We are open to your feedback and happy to answer your questions.

Thank you for your trust, and we wish your child continued success in learning mathematics!

About the author:

Anna Pernal: As a child, her favourite school subject was... of course, math, plus art.! After graduating from architecture, she decided to teach children. She taught architecture, art.,mathematics, and robotics. Her dream is for every child to love math :) She firt tests her books on her own children: John, Andrew and Sophie.

WORLD OF DINOSAURS
COLOR BY MATH
ADDITION & SUBTRACTION

6+

Have a fun with math!

MULTIPLICATION CHART WORKSHEETS TO FILL IN BLANKS

MATH WORKBOOK
TO MEMORIZE TIMES TABLES
FOR 2ND AND 3RD GRADE

MULTIPLICATION WORKBOOK

FOR KIDS

Math practice book to learn and memorize multiplication table for 2nd and 3rd grade.

Made in the USA
Columbia, SC
24 August 2024

41127121R00041